# A Superstar Love Story

*Powering Through the Friend Zone*

Saul Juan Antonio Cuautle

Learn more about Juan Antonio's products, services and
success stories at:
**www.bringbackfit.com**

*To anyone who's ever found themselves stuck in the friend zone.*

*And to my good friend Angelo:*
*Thank you for helping me believe in second chances.*

# CONTENTS

F/9/7/18

Dear Kirsten,

To dreams & hopes of second chances.

I've always found you to be incredibly radiant, caring & charismatic. Having gotten the chance to know you deeper, only magnifies it.

I'm sorry for the tough times you've had to endure. It's not right. But know you are stronger & better because of it.

I hope happiness, peace & love find their home with you again. You're incredible.

Take care,
JA

## 1

## SEEDS OF COURAGE

| JOEY: | *It's never gonna happen.* |
|---|---|
| ROSS: | *What?* |
| JOEY: | *You and Rachel.* |
| ROSS: | *Wha... whatta... What? Why not?* |
| JOEY: | *Because you waited too long to make your move, and now you're in the friend zone.* |
| ROSS: | *No, no, no. I'm not in the zone.* |
| JOEY: | *Ross, you're mayor of the zone.* |

- *Friends,* "The One With The Blackout" (2004)

It takes a great amount of courage for a man weighing 342 pounds to walk into a gym. It takes even more courage to keep coming back. If you've ever stepped inside gym feeling alone, self-conscious or like you didn't belong there, you know exactly what I mean. Please stay the course, because those seeds of courage are only the beginning of your journey. Only time will tell where they'll take you. For my good friend Angelo, they lead him to Jean, the love of his life.

Angelo was a fitness coaching client of mine for a long time. What a lot of people don't know is that I also served as Jean's fitness coach. In fact, we worked together for about six months before she even met Angelo. Having seen her at her best and worst, let me tell you, she's a handful; she speaks her mind, she has a dry sense of humor and she's a health freak - only the finest organic food for her Angelo!

Having had the privilege to work with Jean and Angelo for an extended period of time, and now being able to call them close friends, it's fair to say I've gotten to know them very well over the last few years. I know all their individual dirty secrets and what makes them tick, both inside the gym and out.

I also know they gel together better than Nutella and toast. Even with Angelo as the wizard engineer from Italy and Jean as the workaholic nurse from Ireland, I can honestly say they're very similar. This all you need to know about them: they're good eggs. Meaning, they're caring people.

Some might say they're caring to a fault - "you're too nice" - but in a world where technology is making compassion and kindness harder and harder to find each year, I think having a good heart will only serve to uplift those people in your everyday life. They may be from different parts of the world, with different upbringings, but their heart is from the same mold.

The biggest difference at the time of their meeting was that Jean was super active - hiking, cycling, running, diving, doing CrossFit - while Angelo was in the process of becoming super active.

I've been a fitness coach a long time. Let me tell you a secret nobody knows: I've been trying to get out of coaching almost since the first day I started. I love working with people and helping them reach their goals, but I've always been bothered by how fitness and the idea of exercise operates in the United States. I go in and out of loving and hating it like a dog chasing its tail.

It's either because Jean's a nurse or a redhead, but I think she could sense my restlessness in the gym. She would always send me health and fitness articles highlighting the current state of affairs among the important, but often overlooked, relationship between exercise and medicine. She somehow knew that feeding my mind intellectually is what kept me in the game. As an added bonus, she would send me empowering messages reminding me how important the work I do is.

I can still hear her words, "Your work is the most important factor in this medical-obesity fiasco…. you are literally saving lives in how you can connect with people…how you transform people's lives is priceless…" when I find myself feeling frustrated and wanting to walk away. Her words always hit me at the right time and remind me to focus on my grand vision.

Watch out Angelo, I think it's true what say about redheads - they do have superpowers!

Right before I met Angelo, I was in a period of hating my chosen craft - really hating it. The big corporate gym I was operating in, not only drove me nuts with their red tape, politics, and archaic approaches to fitness, but it was slowly, yet surely, sucking my soul dry.

I couldn't put myself in that environment anymore. I was ready to leave and go do something else - anything else.

On the week I was going to walk away from the corporate gym life, Jean brought Angelo into my life. She met him a few weeks prior at Homemade, a healthy social cooking program they both stumbled into thanks to the magic mix of the internet and busy hospital schedules. During one of the weekly classes, Jean mentioned to Angelo that she had a coach who "always finds a way to kick my ass!"

"Just when I think I have him figured out, he flips the script on me!"

She took it a step further by suggesting Angelo might like training with me. To her surprise, Angelo simply asked, "Where and when should I show up?"

You have no idea how lucky I am. I will be forever grateful for the serendipity that happened between Jean and Angelo over chopping onions and making a fresh kale salad. At that point in my life, when nothing made any sense, Angelo gave me purpose. He's the main reason I stayed on as a coach.

## 2

## *JUST FRIENDS, SILLY*

CHRIS:   *What about Sheila? You making any headway?*

RAY:   *We'll see. I'm taking her to lunch today.*

CHRIS:   *Oh, whoa, whoa whoa. Don't - don't do that. Okay? Don't do lunch.*

RAY:   *Why?*

CHRIS:   *That's like the express lane to the friend zone.*

RAY:   *What the hell's the friend zone?*

CHRIS:   *The friend zone is like the penalty box of dating, only you can never get out. Once a girl decides you're her friend, it's game over. You've become a complete non-sexual entity in her eyes, like her brother, or a lamp.*

*- Just Friends* (2005)

Jean was supposed to meet Angelo on his first visit to the gym. She was going to show him the ins and outs of this huge 4,000+ member complex. Her goal was to show him how this modern day jungle filled with spandex, clunky machines, and loud, club music could be inviting with the right guide.

Angelo's first day was a complete failure. Jean got stuck with patients at the hospital, I was running behind with another client, and the gym staff didn't know who Angelo was since he wasn't a member yet. It wasn't a good first impression for someone who hadn't been to a gym in the United States in almost a decade.

Luckily, Angelo maintained his cool and gave us a chance.

During my first meeting with Angelo, I asked him why he wanted to start exercising - "Why now?" With a sly smile on his face, he said, "I just want to be healthy again. And having more energy would be nice too."

"I'm not fat. I'm fluffy!" That's a term I'm permanently borrowing from stand-up comedian Gabriel Iglesias.

When Angelo and I first met, he was a tad on the "fluffy" side. Let's just say he wore XXX-Large shirts and Jean could comfortably stand inside one half of Angelo's pants. Yes, you read that correctly. We all start somewhere on our fitness journey and that's where Angelo found himself on the fluffy scale.

When I asked him, "On a scale from 1 to 10, how serious are you about your goals?" without hesitation he said, "10. I'm ready. Let's do it."

Instead of jumping for joy, my response was quiet and lukewarm. I was skeptical. I'd become jaded from having had dozens of people tell me this over the years, only to discover they didn't really mean it. Too often, people overestimate their levels of commitment, discipline, and willingness. Their words said one thing, but their actions said something else.

I taught myself to be less interested in what people said and focused more on what they actually did in the real world.

In that silent moment, Angelo had this look in his eyes. This twinkle. It was like he was looking into the future. Whatever he was imagining, I could tell he wanted it more than anything else he'd ever wanted before. I thought he was envisioning himself being leaner, stronger, and healthier, but now I know he was imagining the day he would marry Jean.

When I first saw Jean and Angelo hang out together, they had this energy. This chemistry. Along with their playfulness, I could see there was a deep admiration and respect for each other. I pulled Jean aside and asked her if there was any romantic interest happening.

"God no! We're just friends, silly!"

But as I saw them interact back and forth, I kept thinking, "Jean, are you sure you're just friends? Because I feel like a third wheel interrupting a fourth date."

You'd have to be an idiot not to see something was in the air. Looking at Angelo's face, it was obvious he was smitten like a kitten.

And who can blame him? After all, Jean's beautiful, smart, hardworking, and funny - who doesn't want that in a woman?

Jean was harder to read. I couldn't figure her out. All my detective skills and superhero talents brought back inconclusive evidence.

Where was her heart at? What was she feeling? Thinking?

All I could surmise was that she was fighting herself to hold something back.

Do you want to know what Angelo is like as a friend, man, and husband?

This is all you need to know: Angelo climbed three mountains in Jean's honor. Not one, but three.

.

## 3

# FLUORESCNET YELLOW-GREEN SIGN

*The friend zone, in popular culture, refers to a platonic relationship wherein one person wishes to enter into a romantic or sexual relationship, while the other does not. It is generally considered to be an undesirable or dreaded situation by the lovelorn person. If a desired party does not return or respond affirmatively to the advances or affection of the desiring party, but continues to participate in the friendship in a platonic way, it is sometimes described as friend-zoning.*

- Wikipedia, the free encyclopedia


Jean sent me this text one day: "JUAN ANTONIO! You're not going to believe this!"

She then showed me a picture of Angelo at the top of Mission Peak holding a little sign.

"Angelo is impossible and brilliant! I admire how hard he's working to change. Did you tell him to do this!?"

15

I'll have you know that Mission Peak in Fremont, California is nine miles long and has 5,000ft of elevation to climb. Angelo hiked it just two months into his fitness journey. It took him longer than he projected, he ran out of water, and he took more breaks that most people on the trail, but he made it to the top.

For the record, no, I did not conspire with Angelo to have him climb Mission Peak to impress Jean. He came up with the idea all by himself. I may have helped him get stronger and leaner, but he made it to the top, step-by-step, by his own free will and mental strength.

Angelo intentionally hid his mission from me and kept it on the hush-hush because he knew I wouldn't approve. It's not that I didn't think he wouldn't make it; it was more that I didn't want him to put himself in a position to get injured.

Getting injured is the worst. If you get injured, your fitness journey could easily be derailed for weeks, months, even years. One injury can change everything.

I was afraid Angelo's heart would lead his body down a path it may not have been ready for.

Angelo was no stranger to serious injuries either. He broke his left ankle eight years prior. As a result, he had to get nine pins and a plate installed. And that was before he gained 175 pounds of body fat.

Were those pins designed to handle all that extra load? What about the major joints of the human body?

I was strategically cautious in approaching Angelo's fitness journey because I wanted him to succeed in the long term.

I don't care who you are, or what you're pursuing, you can't rush long term success. Anyone pitching you that overnight success BS is lying to you.

I was upfront with Angelo from day one, "Losing body fat is not a race. Don't treat it like one. It's a process. Time and your level of effort will determine how your journey progresses."

I much prefer to take a step-by-step approach, even if at times, it may appear to be frustratingly "slow."

Additionally, I know all too well about rolling ankles and how they can set you back in your fitness and life goals. I've rolled enough ankles in my lifetime to write a textbook on the subject.

Fortunately for us, Angelo knew his body and heart better than I did.

Jean was so astonished Angelo made it to the top of Mission Peak that she completely overlooked the fluorescent yellow-green sign in his left hand. It was even written in sharpie black ink for emphasis and readability.

Do you know what the sign said?

"For Jean."

Angelo's the type of person that when he sets his mind on something, he goes all in. He had to climb that mountain. Jean started a fire and woke up something inside Angelo that compelled him to vie for her attention. It's like she opened his eyes to a whole new world.

It didn't make logical or fitness training sense for him to attempt to climb Mission Peak, but it felt like the right thing to do in his heart.

He later told me, "Sometimes, you have to do things to prove something."

Whether climbing Mission Peak was to prove something to himself or to Jean, only Angelo knows. Either way, his feat was magical. His sly smile on top of that mountain told me, "This is only the beginning."

When I look at that picture now, my eyes water and I beam with pride at how happy and proud he looked. Positive addictions can strengthen you to overcome your weaknesses.

In climbing Mission Peak, Angelo reminded me that in the battle between mind and body, the mind comes first. We often forget that mental strength isn't just given to us. It's earned by going through various challenges and developing a willingness to step outside our comfort zones. The best and worst part about mental strength is, you're the only one who can put in the necessary work to get it.

## 4

## NO AIR-IN-THE-AIR

*Hey, what you doing with a girl like that?*

*She wears high heels,*
*I wear sneakers.*
*She's cheer captain,*
*And I'm on the bleachers.*
*Dreaming about the day when you wake up and find*
*That what you're looking for has been here the whole time.*

- Taylor Swift, "You Belong With Me", *Fearless* (2008)

Angelo's mental strength and resolve would further be tested during the Rae Lakes Loop trail in Kings Canyon National Park - the home of the third mountain he'd be asked to climb.

The third mountain came to Angelo courtesy of Jean throwing conventional marriage practices out the window.

Jean's no girlie girl. In the make believe land of fashion and makeup, she prefers to sport hiking pants and go all-natural whenever she can.

When you've just logged in a twelve hour shift at the hospital, what do you think is more important, mascara and foundation, or a long shower and getting something to eat?

Jean long outgrew the idea of a white dress, pristine chapel, and knight in shining armor. Give her a good glass of wine and some chocolate and she's one happy lady.

When Jean accepted Angelo's marriage proposal, she had one condition: "We have to get married at Rae Lakes Loop. It's my favorite hike."

She knew a secret spot that had a view to die for. You better believe she got married wearing hiking boots, hiking pants, and with a thirty-pound backpack by her side.

"That's fine Jeanie," Angelo said with assuring confidence.

With all the emotions surrounding a marriage proposal, I'm not sure Angelo knew exactly what he was signing up for. This would be no walk in park as Rae Lakes Loop is one of the most popular hikes in Sequoia and Kings Canyon. It typically takes four to five days to complete the hike. The trail covers 46 miles and begins at an elevation of 5,035 feet.

The name of the third mountain next on Angelo's plate?

Glen Pass. It peaks at an elevation of 11,978 feet.

Angelo would have to successfully climb this mountain on day three if he wanted to get married on day four at the grassy, secret spot Jean had selected. At this point in Angelo's fitness journey, he had lost about eighty pounds of body fat. That's some serious fat loss. Eighty pounds is eighty pounds.

Although he could run, swim, row, lift heavy weights, and was hiking on a weekly basis, the summit would still demand every ounce of physical and mental strength he'd been cultivating with each training session over the last two years.

I affectionately nicknamed the mountain, "Fluffy."

There was a moment of doubt where Angelo questioned if he could actually make it to Glen Pass. We found ourselves in the middle of never ending switchbacks that just seemed like they were a stairway to heaven.

Every time we passed a switchback, you could feel the air getting thinner and thinner. It was depressing. That no-air-in-the-air feeling, combined with a forty-pound backpack you wanted to abandon, an achy back, and feet that longed for a sixty-minute massage, left us demoralized.

I wanted nothing more than to take a hot bath, eat a Zachary's deep dish pizza, and listen to some Taylor Swift.

Angelo wanted nothing more than to turn back. But he knew we'd come too far to turn back now. If we turned back at the halfway point, everything we had done up until then would be for nothing. Being two analytical scientists, we couldn't accept that poor result.

And Angelo knew Jean would kill him, so he snapped out of this negative state and found his motivation real quick.

I'm happy to report that all six members of the hiking party made it safely to the secret wedding spot and back home.

I'll even let you in on some trade secret information: Angelo may have been the fluffiest member of the hiking crew, but he wasn't the slowest member. To say he impressed me is an understatement.

When I think back to how difficult that hike was for so many people on the hiking crew, I marvel at how far Angelo has come with his fitness journey.

One day he's forever stuck inside XXX-Large shirts and the next, he walks in wearing a one X Large shirt with a fifteen-pound weighted vest strapped on for added intensity. If that isn't forward moving progress, I don't know what is.

I only wish more people had the patience to see what progress can look like in the real world.

I'm mentioning this because on day one of the Rae Lakes Loop hike, we ran into some avid hikers on the trail. One of the older and more seasoned hikers had the audacity to tell our lead hiker, Axel, "You're friend Angelo won't make it Glen Pass. He's too big."

Does Angelo still have some body fat to lose before he reaches his ideal, target weight?

Sure. Who doesn't?

But guess what?

Angelo did make it to the top you jerk. He also pulled off a badass wedding ceremony reminiscent of Braveheart too.

In the immortal mannerism invention of Ross Geller from *Friends*, I salute you, Avid Hiker Man, with a horizontal double fist tap - a way of giving you the middle finger without actually having to give it.

Now that Angelo had successfully conquered Fluffy Mountain, you'd think his climbing days were over. Unfortunately, there was a second mountain looming in the shadows, ready to take him down. This would be the most important mountain he'd ever have to climb in his life.

I call it "GSP Mountain."

## 5

# BRAD PITT OF MIXED MARTIAL ARTS

*"You know what's the cool thing about women? Women get to have platonic friends. He's my pal, he's my bud, he's my platonic friend. I love him like a brother. He's my bud, my platonic friend. Men don't have platonic friends okay? We just have women we haven't fucked yet. As soon as I figure this out, I'm in there! I mean, we got some platonic friends, we all do. I mean I got some platonic friends, but they are all by accident. Every platonic friend I got was some woman I was trying to fuck, I made a wrong turn somewhere, and ended up in the friend zone. Oh no, I'm in the friend zone!*

- Chris Rock, *Bring The Pain* (2006)

Angelo had to climb GSP Mountain because of me. You see, I love mixed martial arts. In my fandom, I kept telling Jean she needed to see this highly intelligent and strategic fighter named Georges St-Pierre in action.

"He's known as 'GSP.' He's the Brad Pitt of the mixed

martial arts world. Men want to be him and women want to be with him." I said.

Sure enough, Jean looked him up and discovered that GSP was gorgeous, super fit, and incredibly charismatic.

Sorry for making it more difficult for you Angelo.

Jean once told me, "I bought the most recent Muscle & Fitness magazine because GSP is on the cover. Pathetic, but true."

Haven't we all done this at one point or another?

You have no idea how many magazines I have solely because of the power of Taylor Swift.

Yes, GSP is beautiful on the outside. It's easy to fall in love with his chiseled facial features and Greek god body frame. But in doing so, people tend to overlook how beautiful he is on the inside too. He's kind, humble, modest, hard-working, and fallible. He's the kind of superstar you'd want to have a beer with because he's so down-to-earth.

Call me crazy, but that description sounds a lot like Angelo to me. If you ask his close friends, I'm sure they'd agree.

You know what Jean once told me about GSP?

She said, "He reminds me of the everyday, hardworking people I grew up with in Ireland. I love that he takes care of his parents."

In case you were not aware, GSP grew up in abject poverty to working class parents. He attributed his incredible success in the welterweight division of the UFC to the discipline and love he learned from his parents. Very early in his career, he adopted the mindset that he would strive to work harder than anyone else in the sport.

I love that about GSP.

For those of us who share a similar upbringing, we "get" GSP. His story resonates with us at our core. We've learned that important relationships are not defined by outward appearances. Instead, we care more about the mind. About character. About values.

Seeing GSP succeed at the top of the sport is a reminder that talent is overrated. Passion, along with hard work, when done consistently, will beat out "talent" in nine out of ten cases.

Remember when I mentioned Angelo was a wizard engineer?

I meant it.

Angelo's on another level and the work he does is fascinating, while at the same time, absolutely perplexing. Just imagine talking with Sheldon Cooper from *The Big Bang Theory* television show and you'll have a taste of how my brain feels when I ask Angelo to tell me about his work projects.

Yet, when I asked him how he got so smart, he just gave me his patented sly smile and said, "I just work really hard."

One time, Angelo traveled to Korea for a week of non-stop business meetings and conference lectures. You know what else he was doing during this hectic week?

He was sending me pictures of his treadmill statistics. Being pressed for time or jet lag wouldn't deter him from his mission.

I couldn't help but think, "I've created a monster - THIS GUY IS SUPER SERIOUS!"

When he wasn't lifting weights, he was doing cardio work. When he wasn't doing cardio, he was lifting weights. People that saw him work with me or on his own, referred to him as "a machine." He practically lived in the gym during his attempts to court Jean.

Where did this guy come from?

With the snap of a finger, Angelo even gave up all his wine, cheese, favorite pastas, and Italian sweets. Considering Angelo is 100%, full-blown Italian, this is unheard of! He didn't even protest giving up all his flavorful culture food for power shakes, lean meat, and extra, extra servings of broccoli.

In all my years as a coach, Angelo was the only one

who didn't put up a fight with me over strategic nutrition practices. He simply followed the plan I laid out before him. I've never met someone so motivated. So determined.

Where can I find more people like him?

When I look back at Angelo's fitness records, I feel an incredible sense of accomplishment. A sly smile comes across my face as I realize I have in my hands the blueprint for creating more people like him. I just have to find a way to keep them on the path long enough.

# 6

## TIME IS UP

RAY: *I don't want to be a lamp.*

CHRIS: *Yeah, well then don't be her friend, okay?*
*Take that guy for example...*

[points to a clumsy guy and a gorgeous girl skating
together]

RAY: *You mean that couple?*

CHRIS: *No, I mean the guy that \*wishes\* they were
a couple.*

RAY: *What is your point?*

CHRIS: *My point is - Call Sheila, Ray. Call her
right now. Move your day date to tonight.
Play the entire thing aloof and no matter
what you do, kiss her at the end. 'Cause
friends don't kiss.*

RAY: *How will I know?*

CHRIS: *Look, it doesn't matter. If you feel yourself
going there, walk away.*

RAY: *Where did you come up with this theory?*

CHRIS: *Some chick f'ed me up in high school – bad*

.

*- Just Friends (2005)*

When it comes to relationships, being motivated, determined, and a good person isn't always enough. It's only part of the equation.

We all know how previous relationships can complicate things. The past can muddy the present. During the peak of Angelo's attempts to court Jean, she had an ex-boyfriend come back into her life and turn her world upside down.

That whole ordeal, combined with stress from working long days at the hospital, and Angelo vying for her affection, left Jean emotionally exhausted.

We all have our breaking point and Jean was well passed hers.

One day, out of frustration, she told Angelo, "We are just friends. If you were fit, we could be together."

Angelo was left speechless for days.

Look, I get it. Jean's a nurse, active, and incredibly fit. Of course, she's all about being healthy. But not the "just friends" card!? UGHHHHH. Anything, but that!

Trust me, having been on the receiving end of those words on many occasions, those two words hurt a man's heart like no other. Discovering you've been thrust into the abyss known as the "friend zone" leaves you humiliated, demoralized, and feeling like you want to jump in front of a moving bus.

I was in Los Angeles and I got a text message from Angelo that read:

Time is up my friend. We have lost. She is gone. She has chosen someone else and is avoiding me. I am absolutely serious, I will marry her tomorrow if she felt the same, but there is no more hope for me. I hope she is going to be happy.

I couldn't help but cringe at reading those words. My heart hurt so much for Angelo. The text message was so painful because it brought up old memories of romantic courtships I thought I'd gotten over with. They all of sudden felt so fresh.

As an expert in getting turned down, let me tell you, there is no worse feeling in the world than feeling like you're not enough; like your feelings are rubbish and not worthy of attention. It sucks when you're the only one fighting to keep a relationship alive. But you do it anyway because it feels right.

The downside is it's a rollercoaster of different emotions that flood your life until you can't feel anything. You're left almost empty, numb, gasping for air, just hoping for the one you long for to arrive.

When you love someone with all your heart, they become a part of you. They reside deep within you. In your bones. In your blood. They're on your mind 24/7. They give you life. They give you hope when nothing else does. When you're in that eerie silence in the dark, all alone, all you have is that hope.

What do you do when they leave?

You do the only thing you can. You reach for that hope and you hold on for the rough ride ahead.

Jean is a very giving and supportive person. I saw how painful it was for Angelo not having Jean in his life. She was his bedrock. It's like something was missing inside him. It killed me to see him come into the gym and give that extra look around the room hoping to catch a glimpse of Jean.

I can only imagine how many tears he must have hid behind beads of sweat at not having her around. How heartbroken he must have felt?

He could have quit his fitness journey and I would have understood.

Too many people give up it when it gets really, really, really hard. But Angelo doesn't know how to quit. He's the definition of perseverance. He kept showing up to training sessions and never missed a day at the office. Amazingly, he was never angry or bitter at life. That ability to keep coming back without resentment is why he's my hero.

Who does that? How?

That's why my nickname for Angelo is "Superstar."

Angelo's mother and father obviously did a fantastic job in raising him. If I become half the man he is, the woman I end up with will be blessed.

After weeks of not having Jean in his life, Angelo finally admitted to me that the only reason he was training and losing weight was for Jean.

He asked me, "Am I ridiculous?"

Yes.

But you know what's more ridiculous? Running around in a mask every night thinking you can help people. Or flying around the world thinking you can be a symbol of hope for people who don't even know you. Or thinking you can win a 24-hour race on two bad feet. That's ridiculous.

Angelo, be more ridiculous.

# 7

## THAT HEAD-REST MOVE

*"You have a guy friend, he's a great guy, but you won't date him. Do you know what that's like for the guy? It would be like going on the job interview and [them] say this to you, 'Wow Mr. Perkins, this is a great resume. You got the experience we're looking for. We love your attitude. You're perfect for this job. And we're not going to hire you. We'll probably hire someone who is far less qualified and has a drinking problem. And beats us. But this is great resume. In fact, this is the resume we're going to use to judge all the other candidates. We're not going to hire you ever. Is it okay if we call you every now and then? To complain about the guy we do hire?'"*

- Dwayne Perkins, *Rooftop Comedy* (2010)

Jean eventually admitted to me, "It's not that Angelo's big. It's that he let himself get big. Who let's that happen to them?"

I was so offended she said that; beyond incredibly

31

irritated. I felt like she spit in my face.

I stood there staring through her, breathing deeply, quietly trying to calm myself down. If she had said anything else, I'm certain I would have told her to shut up and to kindly exit the gym.

Luckily for me, she patiently waited for what my answer would be.

I proceeded to tell her, "My entire work as a coach operates on the belief that people can change. I can change. You can change. Everybody can change. I have to believe that. I don't care about the past as much as I care about the present. Changing the body is easy; it's changing the mind that's incredibly hard. Angelo's pushing his limits every day in training; he's shrinking into a new person. On top of that, he's one of a handful of world class research engineers doing genius stuff with lasers and acoustics. That doesn't happen by accident. That takes time, dedication, and not surrendering to challenges at every corner. He's doing all this to be a better person. For you. If you can't see that by now, what are you waiting for? Open. Your. Eyes. The man you've been looking for all your life is right in front of you. Don't lose him."

I then asked Jean to go watch the film *The Last Samurai* starring Tom Cruise. The film has a scene at the end of the second act that's the best cinematic example of love in its purest form.

Without giving too much away, Tom Cruise's character, Nathan Algren, is about to depart for a battle he knows he cannot win. Algren's love interest in the film, Taka, asks Algren to honor her by wearing her dead husband's armor (whom he killed in the first act). The body language and eye contact while she respectfully dresses him is out of this world.

That two minute, thirty-second scene is the most beautiful, non-sexualized love scene you'll ever see. Algren and Taka share one tender kiss and the scene ends with Taka resting her head on Algren's shoulder as she stands close behind him. That head-rest move gets me teary-eyed every time I watch it.

One fleeting touch can pack a lifetime of positive emotions.

So what if Angelo doesn't look like GSP? I don't. And I'm the one who trains for 24 hour races! Only GSP looks like GSP. And Angelo looks like Angelo.

I've seen pictures of Angelo in his glory days - he was a bonafide lady killer. On top of that, he's an amazing chef and builds guitars. That's right, he can build them and play them.

Does this sound like a badass yet?

I think so.

But more than looks, Angelo has cultivated a mind of steel. He has honorable character. He's got more heart than just about anyone I know. Angelo doesn't know this, but he reminds me of my dad in how kind and sweet he is. I love that about him.

Please don't ever lose that Angelo. That never goes out of style.

## 8

## WORTH FIGHTING FOR

*Think I know where you belong*
*Think it's with me*

*Can't you see*
*That I'm the one*
*Who understands you?*
*Been here all along.*
*So, why can't you see*
*You belong with me.*

- Taylor Swift, "You Belong With Me", *Fearless* (2008)

$Y$es, physical attraction and chemistry are important to any romantic relationship, but physical attraction can be a tricky bastard. It's not always real. It can lie to you. It can lead you down an unfulfilling path.

At its best, it changes when you change.

Fast forward thirty-nine years. When you're soft, wrinkly, and slow, what's going to hold your marriage together?

If you think it's withered six-pack abs or chiseled facial features, please don't bother getting married. You're only setting yourself up for a costly, rude awakening.

The core of any serious relationship should be a strong and deeply rooted friendship. If that friendship allows for genuine laughter, endless support, and someone who lets you be yourself, then you'll always be in good company.

Jean and Angelo have that.

At the end of the day, Jean is in Angelo's corner, no matter what. Likewise, he guards her heart at all costs. Don't we all want that?

Loyalty and affection like that are very rare. It mostly happens in movies. If you ever find it in real life, cherish it and don't let it slip away. You'll hate yourself for a long time if you do.

The truth isn't always obvious. It takes time to brew to the surface.

Sometimes, your silly preferences get in your own way. When you're brave enough to confront your long held preferences face-to-face, you can either blindly commit to them, or you can look at the bigger picture and sidestep intentionally.

When you find yourself wanting to spend all your time with someone; when that person makes any situation more enjoyable; when you feel like you can tell that person anything; when that person knows more about you than anyone else in the world and the relationship gets tough, you know what you do?

You fight for that person.

You take a chance and put it all on the line. You give the best part of you because that person may only come around once in a lifetime. Someone like that is worth fighting for.

All the setbacks, all the rejection, and all the "no's"

suddenly become irrelevant. You take the pain. You go into the pain. You endure the pain. You become a better person because of that pain.

The genius of Angelo's mind is that he never gave up. He found a way to hold on when most of us would have let go.

It's amazing how strong you can be when you have no other option than to be strong.

I'll tell you a secret. As Angelo was holding on, I was sending Jean little quotes, videos, and music that probably confused her. Was I cheering Angelo on?

Of course, he's my dude.

Was I trying to help Jean through a slump?

Absolutely. I had inside knowledge, but I couldn't speak for Angelo or Jean. And I couldn't do the necessary work for them. They had to connect the dots on their own.

All I did was try to return the favor by reminding Jean of her own words. I encouraged her to look beyond right now and see the bigger picture.

Did it have an impact?

Maybe.

All I know is that after many weeks of not having seeing Jean, Angelo wrote a beautiful letter during a really tough time in Jean's life. To quote Jean, "He is very eloquent. He's brought me to tears. And he drives me nuts!"

Angelo, for the love of all that is holy, please tell me what you wrote! I need to know the contents of that letter. Millions of men around the world need to know how you cracked the code and powered through the friend zone!

Kudos to whoever understands women.

I can't tell you what was in that letter. Maybe it's only for Angelo and Jean to know?

But I can tell you that this entire love story can be summarized with these lines:

*Love is patient. Love is kind. It does not envy. It does not boast.*

*It is not proud. It does not dishonor others. It is not self-seeking. It is not easily angered. It keeps no records of wrongs. Love does not delight in evil, but rejoices in the truth. It always protects, always trusts, always hopes, always perseveres.*

Angelo's journey embodies this message.

Thank you for showing me the way my friend. Thank you for showing me you'll never know what you're truly capable of until you give more than you're capable of giving. Thank you for showing me it's okay to be "ridiculous."

And Jean, thank you for not giving up on me.

As you embark on new marriage adventures and climb new mountains together, I hope you hold hands every step of the way. Keep each other ever close and rest your head on each other's shoulder. Grow that positive addiction and let it show you how powerful you can be together.

I offer you these last words as a blessing. Like you, they always bring a smile to my face:

*May the road rise up to meet you.*
*May the wind always be at your back.*
*May the sun shine warm upon your lovely faces,*
*And rains fall soft upon your fields.*
*And may the wings of destiny, carry your love to dance with the stars.*

# ACKNOWLEDGEMENTS

First and foremost, thank you Angelo and Jean for welcoming me into your lives. You were model clients. I'm honored to have had the chance to work with you. I'm proud to call you friends. I'll never forget your generosity and friendship. There would be no Superstar Love Story without you.

Thanks to mom and dad, for showing me what discipline, hard work, and sacrifice look like.

To the multi-talented Chris Sanchez, one of my closest and longest standing friends. You are family. You've seen me at my best and at my worst. Thank you for always asking the hard questions and challenging me to think long and hard about issues encountered in bringing my creations to life. Some of my best stuff comes out through your continued pressings to dig deeper. Thanks bro. I love you.

To my fabulous supercoach Krista Scott-Dixon. Thank you for reminding me to harness, leverage, and work on my superpowers on daily basis. You are dearly missed.

To my college roommate Ranjeet Jhutti. Thanks for giving me a chance to express my doubts, fears, and frustrations with you about the startup life. And for helping me laugh when all I want to do is cry.

To videographer extraordinaire Alyssa "Pinky" Glidewell. Thank you for your patience in my quest for storytelling perfection. And for all your hard work in helping me tell better stories. Your two cents are always welcomed and appreciated.

To Jeff Bezos, founder and CEO of Amazon.com. Thank you for betting on yourself and your vision. Your technical wonders and continued innovations have enabled me to publish this book. Also, your "regret minimization framework" is pure genius.

My sincerest gratitude to Gina Morra Smith. Thank you for your insightful feedback on all my projects. Your ever present support and encouragement mean more than you know.

To my kindergarten teacher Mrs. H. Florence Kubota. Thank you for patiently teaching me and all my siblings after me, how to get our thoughts on paper. You were the first person to identify my storytelling abilities. Thank you for pushing me to get out in front of everyone when all I wanted to do was stay quiet.

To Olatunde "Tunde" Sobomehin, your passion and genuineness are infectious. Your work with StreetCode Academy in East Palo Alto, California inspires me to be a better person every day. Thank you for making me feel like family. I'm humbled by your kindness. Thank you for sparking and renewing my love for the underprivileged and underserved.

Special thanks to Theodore "Tad" Schink. I wouldn't have made it this far without your endless and continued support. Thank you for believing in me and helping me bring my vision to reality. I owe you a huge debt of gratitude.

And to my favorite superstar: Taylor Alison Swift. Your magical presence, radiant positive energy, and beautiful mind never fail to bring me joy and make me smile. I can't tell you how many times your voice has inspired me to continue working on my projects. Whenever I feel I can't take it anymore, you help me not to break. You remind me to get back up every time I fall apart. You show me how to keep going. My writing wouldn't be possible without your guiding light. Thank you, Taylor.

JUAN ANTONIO

# Q&A ABOUT THE BOOK

*Why did you write this book?*

There are a lot of lonely people out there looking for companionship. And I don't care what anyone says, all those people looking for relationships want to experience genuine love. They want to hold onto somebody and not let go. But finding love isn't as simple as swiping right, double tapping a heart, or sending someone a digital wink.

If you want to find real love, it's going to take effort, time, and plenty of patience.

We live in an interesting time where technology is changing the nature and dynamics of relationships - especially romantic relationships. With the click of a few buttons, you could be meeting a potential new mate that same day!

Sure, all the dating websites and mobile apps are making "dates" more accessible for people living in a busy world, and "dates" can lead to relationships, but people are forgetting how to relate to each other by relying too much on this same technology to do the heavy lifting for them.

Although technology has its place, no mobile app will ever be able to engage in crucial conversations for you.

You can only hide behind technology for so long. At some point, those technological walls will come down and you'll have that special person right in front of you. In that moment, you'll have to use your own mouth, own words, and body language to communicate.

I think too many people forget that. In forgetting that, they choose the path of inaction and let too many opportunities pass them by.

Ideally, this story will help remind people that the quality of your life is directly related to the quality of your communication with those closest to you. And that you have to risk taking a chance to get what you want.

Also, it seems the friend zone is pretty universal.

Almost everyone has either put someone in the friend zone or been put in the friend zone by someone. It's a human nature thing.

Every time someone would come to me with their dating woes, challenges or lack-of-a-dating life, I'd tell them some aspect of Angelo's story and they'd walk away feeling empowered and hopeful about their relationship or prospects of future relationships.

Seeing those smiles on their faces told me the story had a valuable message for all those people hovering in and around the friend zone. I wanted to find a way to scale that hopeful message and boom, the book came to fruition.

*What inspired you to write this book?*

I was Angelo's best man for the wedding at Rae Lakes Loop. I was pleasantly surprised when he walked into the gym one day and just slyly mentioned, "What do you think about being the best man?"

Since there would only be six people in attendance for the ceremony - including the bride and groom - I didn't bother preparing a traditional best man speech. Having been a best man twice before, I was thoroughly relieved.

In fact, at the hike wedding ceremony, everyone was so hungry and tired, that we completely overlooked speeches all together.

Jean and Angelo decided to have a party to celebrate the wedding. It would be held in Angelo's home town of Monopoli, Italy.

For some reason, I didn't consider myself an international best man. I thought I signed up to be the best man only in the United States. In my mind, I just had to show up for the wedding during the hike, not the party to celebrate the wedding.

When my client Karina pointed out my grave mistake, I freaked out and realized a) I needed to find a way to get to Italy, b) most of the audience members would be native Italian speakers, and c) a best man speech would probably be in expected.

Long story short, the budget was too tight for me to attend the party in Monopoli, Italy. I felt terrible for not being in attendance.

What kind of best man misses the wedding party?

To make up for my absence, I decided to write an epic best man speech and have it translated in Italian as my gift to Jean and Angelo. I originally planned on doing a live reading via Skype, but I discovered that I read painstakingly slow in Italian.

Although the content was good, the delivery would have been terrible. Shave this book down about 13 pages and you'll get a version of the best man speech I wrote.

Yeah, I know, too long.

Everything I took out to make the speech work, I put back in. Everything that wouldn't make sense in a speech format, would work in a book format.

Essentially, you can consider the book like an expanded *Lords of the Rings* "director's cut" of the epic best man speech. But in its expanded format, it can serve as a gift to everyone who's ever had to deal with the bittersweet nature of romantic relationships.

*What would you like your readers to take away from your book?*

Angelo told me the best man speech went over very well with the family in Monopoli. "You made me cry JA," were his exact words.

Depending on where you find yourself in your relationship journey, your fitness journey, or your personal transformation journey, will dictate what part of the story speaks to you the most.

That, combined with whether you're looking for a relationship, are in a happy relationship, are in an unsatisfying relationship, or are happily single, will bring out different emotions and desires.

I'd love it if the book got people thinking about why they have the preferences they have.

*Why do I like-slash-want-slash-love person X?*

To our own detriment, we can be very focused on physical attributes in romantic relationships. I hope more people develop an awareness and appreciation for character values and personality traits.

Do you remember the ending scene of the film *Good Will* Hunting where Robin Williams' character Sean McGuire reads Will's note?

"If the professor calls about that job, tell him I had to go see about a girl."

Every time I watch that scene, I want to stand and raise my fist in triumph like Sylvester Stallone at the end of the training montage in the motion picture *Rocky Balboa*.

Love can be a scary thing and any time someone dares enough to takes a chance, it's a win. I hope the story can create more triumph moments for people.

As well, do you remember the final scene in the film *The Pursuit of Happyness*, where Chris Gardner gets offered a job with the brokerage firm?

I cry without fail, every, single, time. And you know

what?

It feels good. It's a good cry. I hope some people get to experience a good cry at some point during the story.

Lastly, if someone gets inspired enough to decide they want to transform their body by changing their eating patterns and exercise habits, I'll take that as a big win. And if someone else decides to take a chance to get out of the friend zone - win, lose or draw - I'll take that as a big win too.

I love when people try, even if they fail.

*What was the hardest part about writing this book?*

First of all, it was deciding that I wanted to put the story out there. When I finished the best man speech, I wasn't 113% happy with it. It was good, but I felt like I left out so much great material. It felt incomplete to me. When I made the decision to go all-in and expand the story, I got a second chance to complete the story to my satisfaction.

Then it was the editing. Editing is difficult for me because I obsess over every single little detail in my creations. Everything counts. Everything matters. It doesn't get easier for me, but the more time I spend doing it, the more confident I become with why I placed everything where I placed it. Eventually, I reach a state of contentment and let go of the editing phase.

The hardest part was definitely how I structured the story.

Right from paragraph one, I gave away a critical piece of information: "lead him to the love of his life."

If you picked up on that hint, you know the story has a happy ending. I had to find a way to build the drama and suspense in an interesting and entertaining way even though I let the cat out the bag.

I initially felt like I couldn't start out my story like that. "It should end like that" a part of me kept thinking. But trying to write the story with that ending in mind didn't work. The story sucked.

I tried approaching it from various angles, but I couldn't make the story work. It didn't feel right. That structure felt very unnatural and I really felt like I was doing the story a disservice. I was forcing a story that even I didn't want to read.

Forget writer's block, this was "your story sucks" land.

I made a breakthrough in trusting my original structure after taking inspiration from the film Titanic. In that film, you know the ship is going down, but you don't know how all the events meet together to make the ending work.

After watching the film again, I gained confidence that my structure, although odd, was the way to go for how I wanted to tell the story. I finally stopped fighting myself. That trusting-your-gut moment was the true turning point in the story. After that, it all started flowing together.

# ABOUT THE AUTHOR

Saul Juan Antonio Cuautle is a writer, coach, and tech entrepreneur based out of Menlo Park, CA. He's the Founder & CEO of Minds of Steel—a tech startup building fitness coaching software that helps you "Discover Your Inner Superhero." When he's not studying business, design, or learning mobile programming, he can be found reading non-fiction books, watching films that move him, and embedding himself in the world of mixed martial arts. He prefers to be addressed by his middle name, Juan Antonio. Yes, you have to say both names.

Learn more about him and his journey at **www.bringbackfit.com**

# OTHER BOOKS BY JUAN ANTONIO

*Long Live: Beating Cancer Through Happyness and Selfies*

# ASKING FOR YOUR HELP...

*Please honor the Angelo and Jean's of the world. People need to know about their daring efforts.*

If know your time is limited, so thank you for your time, attention, and consideration in reading this book. If you enjoyed this story, and found it of value, I ask you to please help the book by leaving a review on Amazon.com

It may not seem like much, but your support does make a world of difference in the success of this book. I can't get through the noise and Amazon's book algorithms alone.

I read all the reviews personally, and take your feedback into consideration to make this book and future stories even better.

As well, please help share the message forward by telling your friends, family, and people in your life whom you care about. Please help spread the word on social media.

Your thoughtfulness in helping me reach more people is very much appreciated.

If I can be of any assistance, or if you have more questions you want added to the Q&A, please feel free to send an email to **ja@bringbackfit.com**.

I wish you much success on your relationship journey. Keep. Going. Thank you again for your support. I'll see you on the flipside.

Take care,

– JA

Made in the USA
San Bernardino, CA
03 June 2018